WELCOME TO THE ENCHANTING WORLD OF COCKTAILS, WHERE EACH DRINK IS A SPELL!
TO UNLOCK THE FULL MAGIC OF THE COCKTAIL, YOU NEED NOT ONLY MIX THE PERFECT INGREDIENTS BUT ALSO BRING THEM TO LIFE WITH A SPECIAL TOAST—YOUR INCANTATION.
REMEMBER, YOUR EMOTIONS AND SENSATIONS ARE THE KEY TO CREATING WONDERS.
DISCOVER THE ART OF COCKTAIL MAGIC AND ENJOY EVERY MOMENT OF THIS CAPTIVATING JOURNEY!

TO OUR INSATIABLE THIRST FOR ADVENTURE - MAY OUR JOURNEYS
BE FILLED WITH MAGIC AND MYSTERIES, LIKE AN ENCHANTED
FOREST.
AND LET THIS DRINK BE LIKE A LIGHT IN THE DARK FOREST, GUIDING
US THROUGH THE MYSTERIOUS SHADOWS TO A JOYFUL DAWN.
WITH EACH SIP, WE DISCOVER NEW PATHS, AND WITH EACH STEP,
WE DRAW CLOSER TO THE WARM LIGHT THAT PROMISES
NEW BEGINNINGS.
TO ADVENTURES THAT WARM THE HEART!

ENCHANTED FOREST MOJITO

50 ML OF LIGHT RUM
30 ML OF FRESHLY SQUEEZED LIME JUICE
2 TEASPOONS OF MAGICAL SUGAR CRYSTALS
8-10 MINT LEAVES FROM A NOBLE BUSH
SODA FROM A PURE SPRING

ICE

PREPARATION:

IN A SACRED GOBLET, PLACE THE MINT LEAVES AND MAGICAL
SUGAR CRYSTALS.
DRIZZLE THEM WITH FRESHLY SQUEEZED LIME JUICE FROM THE TREE OF
WISDOM AND ADD THE ELIXIR OF LIGHT RUM.
STIR THE MAGICAL MIXTURE, ADD ICE CRYSTALS, AND TOP UP WITH
SODA FROM A PURE SPRING.
GARNISH YOUR CREATION WITH A SPRIG OF MINT FROM THE NOBLE
BUSH AND A SLICE OF LIME TO ADD EVEN MORE MAGIC.

LET'S DRINK TO THE DRAGON'S POWER WITHIN US - IT ALLOWS US TO OVERCOME OBSTACLES AND SHINE BRIGHTER THAN THE STARS IN THE SKY!
MAY THEIR LIGHT BE WITH US!

THE BIRTH OF THE DRAGON

60 ML WHISKEY
30 ML VERMOUTH
2 DROPS OF BITTERS
ICE

PREPARATION:

IN A SACRED SHAKER, MIX THE WHISKEY POTION, HOLY VERMOUTH, AND TWO DROPS OF MYSTICAL BITTERS WITH AN ICE CRYSTAL. SHAKE VIGOROUSLY TO AWAKEN THE SPIRITS OF MAGIC. STRAIN INTO A CHILLED COCKTAIL GLASS. GARNISH WITH A TWIST OR CHERRY, ADDING AN EXTRA TOUCH OF ENCHANTMENT TO THE DRINK.

CONSUME IN THE MOST PLEASANT ATMOSPHERE TO FEEL THE UNFORGETTABLE MOMENT OF THE DRAGON'S BIRTH, PRECISELY AT THAT MOMENT WHEN THE WARMTH OF THE DRINK SPREADS THROUGH YOUR BODY FROM THE FIRST SIPS. DO YOU FEEL IT? THAT IS YOUR DRAGON. MAY ITS STRENGTH AND WISDOM BE WITH YOU.

TO THE MAGIC OF THE MOMENT WHEN DREAMS BECOME REALITY,
AND REALITY BECOMES A FAIRY TALE FILLED WITH MAGIC AND
WONDERS!

MYSTERIOUS ISLAND PIÑA COLADA

60 ML WHITE RUM
90 ML PINEAPPLE JUICE
30 ML COCONUT CREAM
ICE

PREPARATION:

IN THE WITCHES' CASTLE, HIDDEN AMONG THE MISTS, MIX THE WHITE RUM ELIXIR, PINEAPPLE JUICE FROM THE ENCHANTED GARDEN, AND COCONUT CREAM FROM THE MAGICIANS' ASSEMBLY IN A BOWL WITH ICE CRYSTALS FROM MAGICAL ICE.
BLEND THE MIXTURE UNTIL SMOOTH AND POUR INTO A COCONUT GLASS.
GARNISH YOUR PIÑA COLADA WITH A PIECE OF PINEAPPLE, WHICH CAN OPEN THE DOORS TO THE MYSTERIOUS WORLD OF MAGIC AND WONDERS.

DRINK TO THE MAGIC OF FRIENDSHIP, WHICH, LIKE A MAGICAL BOND, UNITES OUR HEARTS INTO ONE AND MAKES US STRONGER AND MORE CONFIDENT, LIKE TRUE WIZARDS READY TO OVERCOME ANY OBSTACLES AND CHALLENGES!

COSMIC COSMOPOLITAN

45 ML VODKA

15 ML TRIPLE SEC

15 ML FRESHLY SQUEEZED LIME JUICE

30 ML CRANBERRY JUICE

PREPARATION:

IN THE CASTLE OF THE GREAT MAGICIANS, MIX THE MAGICAL VODKA DRINK, ANCIENT TRIPLE SEC, FRESHLY SQUEEZED LIME JUICE FROM THE ASTRAL SPHERES, AND CRANBERRY JUICE FROM THE ENCHANTED FIELD.

CREATE A MAGICAL CHARGE IN THE SHAKER BY SHAKING IT VIGOROUSLY. STRAIN THE MIXTURE INTO A CHILLED COCKTAIL GLASS. GARNISH WITH A LIME WHEEL OR CRANBERRY TO BRING MAGIC TO EVERY SIP.

TO OUR ABILITY TO FIND MAGIC IN THE MOST ORDINARY MOMENTS OF LIFE AND MAKE THEM SPECIAL! TO OUR INDOMITABLE THIRST FOR LIFE - MAY EVERY DAY BE AN ADVENTURE, AND EVERY EVENING A MIRACLE!

MYSTERIOUS SORCERER'S OLD-FASHIONED

50 ML BOURBON OR RUM
1 SUGAR CUBE
2 DROPS OF ANGOSTURA BITTERS
ICE CRYSTALS FROM A MAGICAL SOURCE

PREPARATION:

IN THE TOWER OF THE SAGE, WHERE THE WISDOM OF THE AGES IS KEPT, RUB THE MAGICAL SUGAR CRYSTAL WITH ANCIENT ANGOSTURA.
ADD ICE CRYSTALS FROM THE MAGICAL SOURCE AND POUR IN THE ANCIENT BOURBON OR RUM FROM THE LOST BOOKS.
STIR THE MIXTURE THOROUGHLY, ACTIVATING THE MAGICAL PROP-ERTIES.

TO OUR MAGIC OF LOVE, WHICH, LIKE A SPELL, TRANSFORMS THE GRAY WEEKDAYS INTO A CELEBRATION AND FILLS OUR HEARTS WITH WARMTH AND LIGHT, LIKE A MAGICAL LANTERN IN THE DARK NIGHT!

MAGICAL LOVEGARITA

45 ML OF TEQUILA POTION
30 ML OF LEMON JUICE
15 ML OF ORANGE LIQUEUR
ICE

PREPARATION:

ELEMENTAL MAGIC SALT FOR RIMMING THE GLASS (OPTIONAL)
IN A FAIRY-TALE SHAKER, MIX THE TEQUILA POTION, LEMON JUICE,
AND ORANGE LIQUEUR WITH ICE.
SHAKE VIGOROUSLY TO ACTIVATE THE MAGICAL PROPERTIES.
STRAIN INTO A CHILLED COCKTAIL GLASS, HAVING RIMMED THE
EDGE WITH ELEMENTAL MAGIC SALT IF DESIRED.
GARNISH WITH A SLICE OF LIME OR ORANGE, ADDING AN EXTRA
TOUCH OF ENCHANTMENT TO THE GLASS. AND REMEMBER, ONLY
YOUR BURNING HEART CAN ACTIVATE THE SUPERPOWER OF YOUR
DRINK. CREATE WITH LOVE!

DRINK TO THE MAGIC WITHIN EACH OF US, WHICH, LIKE A MAGIC WAND, ALLOWS US TO TRANSFORM THE WORLD AROUND US AND MAKE IT BRIGHTER, MORE COLORFUL, AND MEMORABLE, LIKE A MAGICAL WATERCOLOR LANDSCAPE!

MAGICAL DAIQUIRI

60 ML OF RUM
30 ML OF FRESHLY SQUEEZED LIME JUICE
15 ML OF MANGO SYRUP
ICE

PREPARATION:

IN AN ENCHANTED SHAKER, COMBINE THE LIGHT RUM ELIXIR,
ESSENCE OF FRESHLY SQUEEZED LIME JUICE, AND MANGO SYRUP
FROM THE TREE OF WISDOM WITH AN ICE CRYSTAL.
SHAKE TO ACTIVATE THE MAGICAL PROPERTIES.
STRAIN INTO A CHILLED COCKTAIL GLASS.
GARNISH WITH A LIME WEDGE OR A SMALL AMULET FIGURE.
REMEMBER, A DRINK CONSUMED IN THE COMPANY OF AT LEAST
SEVEN FRIENDS ENHANCES YOUR LUCK FOR AN ENTIRE YEAR!

TO OUR MAGICAL SENSE OF INSPIRATION, WHICH, LIKE A MAGICAL FIRE, IGNITES THE FLAME OF CREATIVITY IN OUR HEARTS AND ALLOWS US TO CREATE OUR OWN WORLDS AND STORIES, FULL OF MAGIC AND FANTASY!

MAGICAL MAI TAI

45 ML OF LIGHT RUM
30 ML OF FRESHLY SQUEEZED LIME JUICE
15 ML OF ORANGE LIQUEUR
15 ML OF ALMOND SYRUP
15 ML OF DARK RUM
ICE

PREPARATION:

IN A MAGICAL SHAKER, MIX THE LIGHT RUM POTION, ESSENCE OF
FRESHLY SQUEEZED LIME JUICE, ORANGE LIQUEUR, ALMOND SYRUP,
AND DARK RUM ELIXIR WITH AN ICE CRYSTAL.
SHAKE VIGOROUSLY TO AWAKEN THE MAGICAL ENERGY.
UTTER THE ENCHANTING SPELL: "CHARMING," TO ACTIVATE YOUR
OWN ATTRACTIVENESS. STRAIN INTO A CHILLED COCKTAIL GLASS.
GARNISH WITH A MINT SPRIG AND AN ORANGE SLICE, ADDING
EXTRA MAGIC TO THE DRINK. BUT REMEMBER, EXCESSIVE ALCOHOL
CONSUMPTION WILL TURN YOUR CARRIAGE INTO A PUMPKIN.

TO OUR MAGICAL UNION OF SOULS - MAY OUR LOVE BE LIKE A
SORCERER'S SPELL THAT WARMS OUR HEARTS AND PROTECTS US
FROM EVIL!

BLOODY GHOST MARY

50 ML OF VODKA
120 ML OF TOMATO JUICE
15 ML OF FRESHLY SQUEEZED LIME JUICE
2 DROPS OF WORCESTERSHIRE SAUCE
SEASONING FROM ENCHANTING HERBS

PREPARATION:

IN A SUPERNATURAL SHAKER, MIX THE VODKA POTION, TOMATO JUICE, FRESHLY SQUEEZED LIME JUICE, AND TERRIFYING WORCESTER-SHIRE SAUCE WITH AN ICE CRYSTAL. SHAKE.

TO THE MAGIC OF WORDS AND PROMISES - MAY EACH OF OUR WORDS BE A WORD OF WISDOM AND KINDNESS, FILLING OUR HEARTS WITH JOY AND PROSPERITY!

MAGICAL TEQUILA SUNRISE

45 ML OF TEQUILA
30 ML OF ORANGE JUICE
15 ML OF GRENADINE SYRUP
ICE

PREPARATION:

IN A SPELLBINDING SHAKER, MIX THE TEQUILA POTION, ESSENCE OF ORANGE LIGHT, AND MAGICAL GRENADINE SYRUP WITH AN ICE CRYSTAL OF MORNING DEW.
SHAKE VIGOROUSLY TO ACTIVATE THE MAGICAL PROPERTIES.
STRAIN INTO A CHILLED COCKTAIL GLASS.
ADD A DROP OF MAGICAL FIRE AND WATCH AS YOUR TEQUILA SUNRISE BEGINS TO GLOW.

TO OUR MAGICAL SENSE OF LOVE, WHICH, LIKE A MAGICAL FIRE,
IGNITES THE FLAME OF PASSION, CREATIVITY IN OUR HEARTS AND
ALLOWS US TO CREATE OUR OWN WORLDS AND STORIES, FULL OF
MAGIC AND FANTASY.

SEX ON THE BEACH MAGIC

45 ML OF VODKA POTION
30 ML OF MYSTICAL CRANBERRY JUICE
30 ML OF PEACH ELIXIR
45 ML OF HOLY POMEGRANATE MIX
ICE FROM THE FROZEN DRAGON'S BREATH

PREPARATION:

IN A MYSTERIOUS SHAKER, MIX THE VODKA POTION, MYSTICAL CRANBERRY JUICE, PEACH ELIXIR, AND HOLY POMEGRANATE MIX WITH AN ICE CRYSTAL.
SHAKE TO MIX THE INGREDIENTS AND ACTIVATE THE MAGICAL POWER. STRAIN INTO A CHILLED COCKTAIL GLASS. GARNISH WITH AN ORANGE SLICE AND A MAGICAL POMEGRANATE BERRY.

TO OUR MAGICAL IMAGINATION, WHICH TURNS OUR DREAMS INTO VIVID REALITY AND GIVES US THE OPPORTUNITY TO BECOME THE FAIRY-TALE HEROES OF OUR OWN STORY!

MAGICAL LONG ISLAND

15 ML OF VODKA
15 ML OF TEQUILA
15 ML OF LIGHT RUM
15 ML OF SEC
15 ML OF LEMON LIGHT
30 ML OF SUGAR CANE SYRUP
30 ML OF LEMON JUICE
60 ML OF DIVINE CARBONATED WATER
ICE

PREPARATION:

IN A MYSTERIOUS SHAKER, MIX THE POTIONS OF VODKA, TEQUILA, LIGHT RUM, SEC, ESSENCE OF LEMON LIGHT, MAGICAL SUGAR CANE SYRUP, AND HOLY LEMON JUICE WITH AN ICE CRYSTAL OF ARCTIC ICE. ADD DIVINE CARBONATED WATER AND SHAKE WITH MAGICAL ENERGY.
STRAIN INTO A CHILLED COCKTAIL GLASS. GARNISH WITH AN ORANGE SLICE, A LEMON WEDGE, AND FRESH BERRIES TO GIVE YOUR DRINK A MAGICAL AURA.